NATIONAL GEOGRAPHIC

Taking Care of Farm Animals

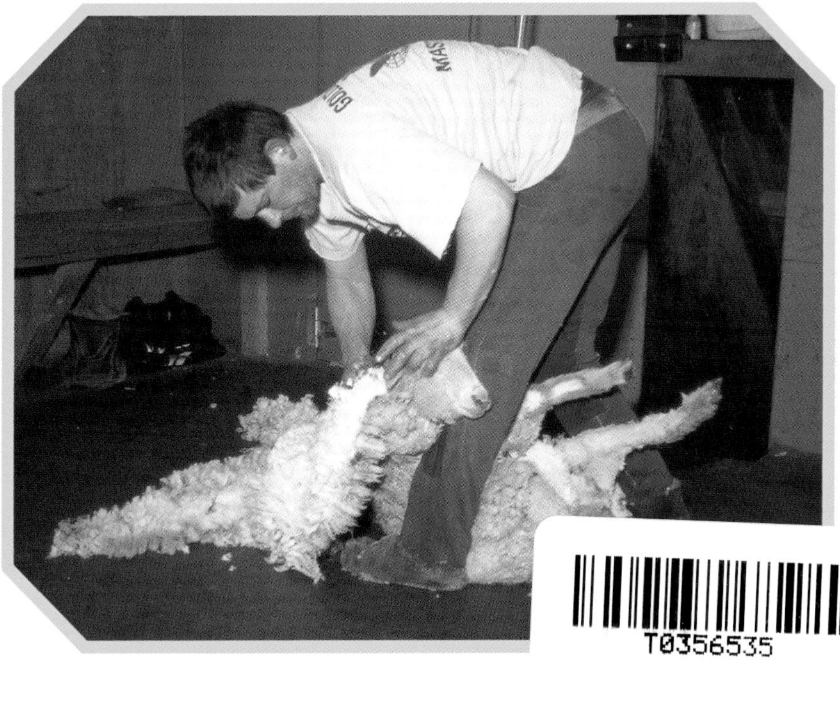

T0356535

Dimi Stanos

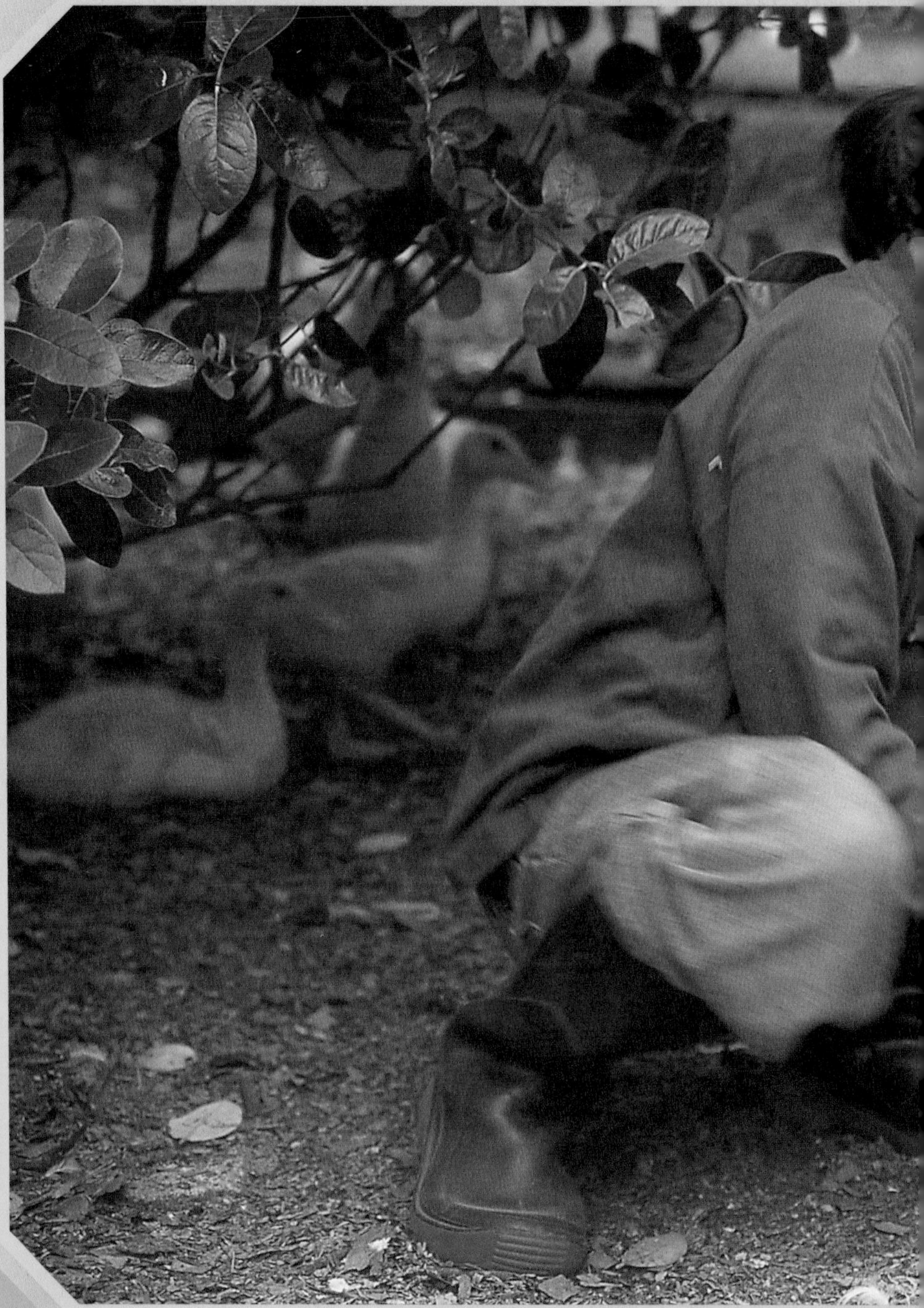

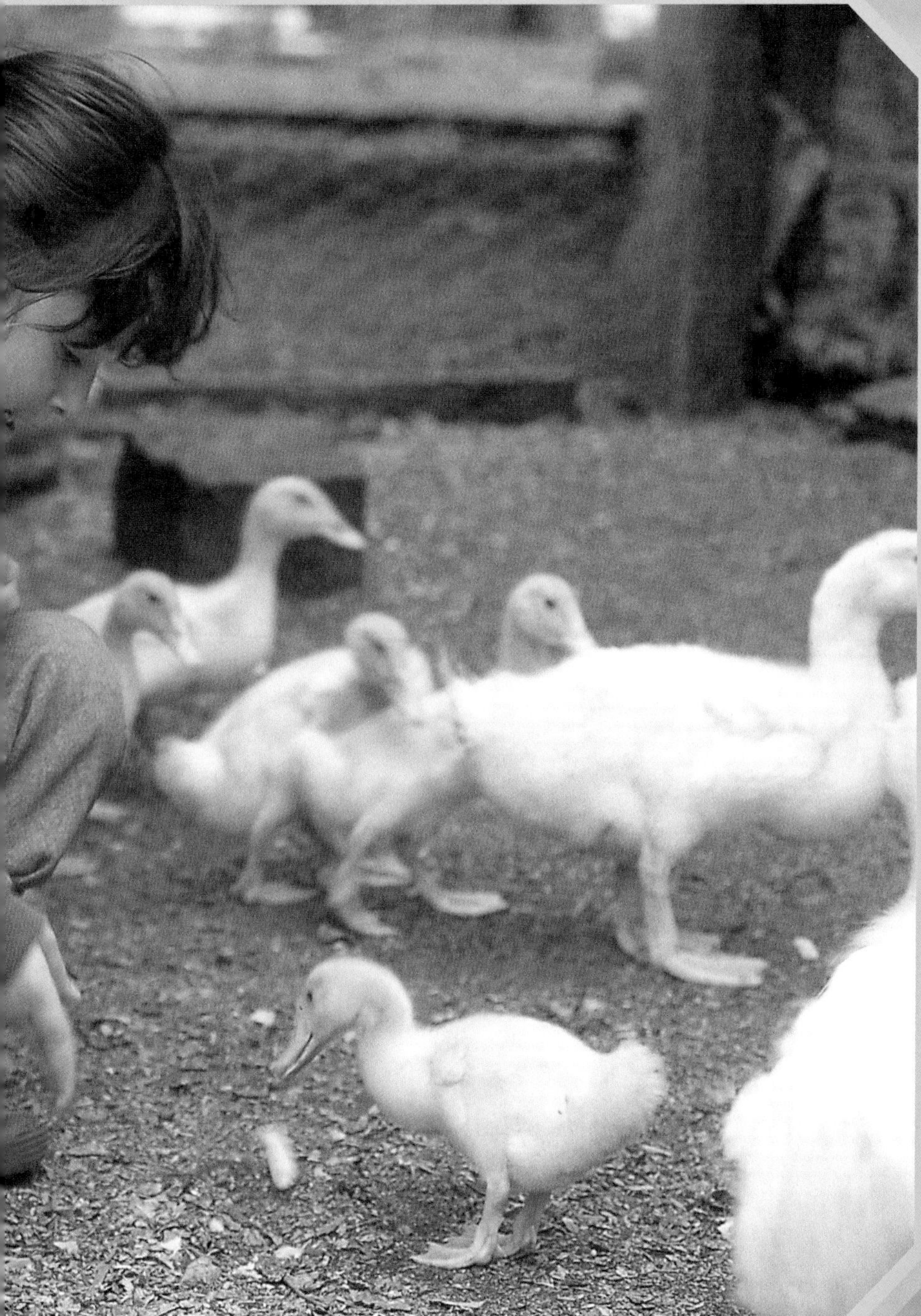

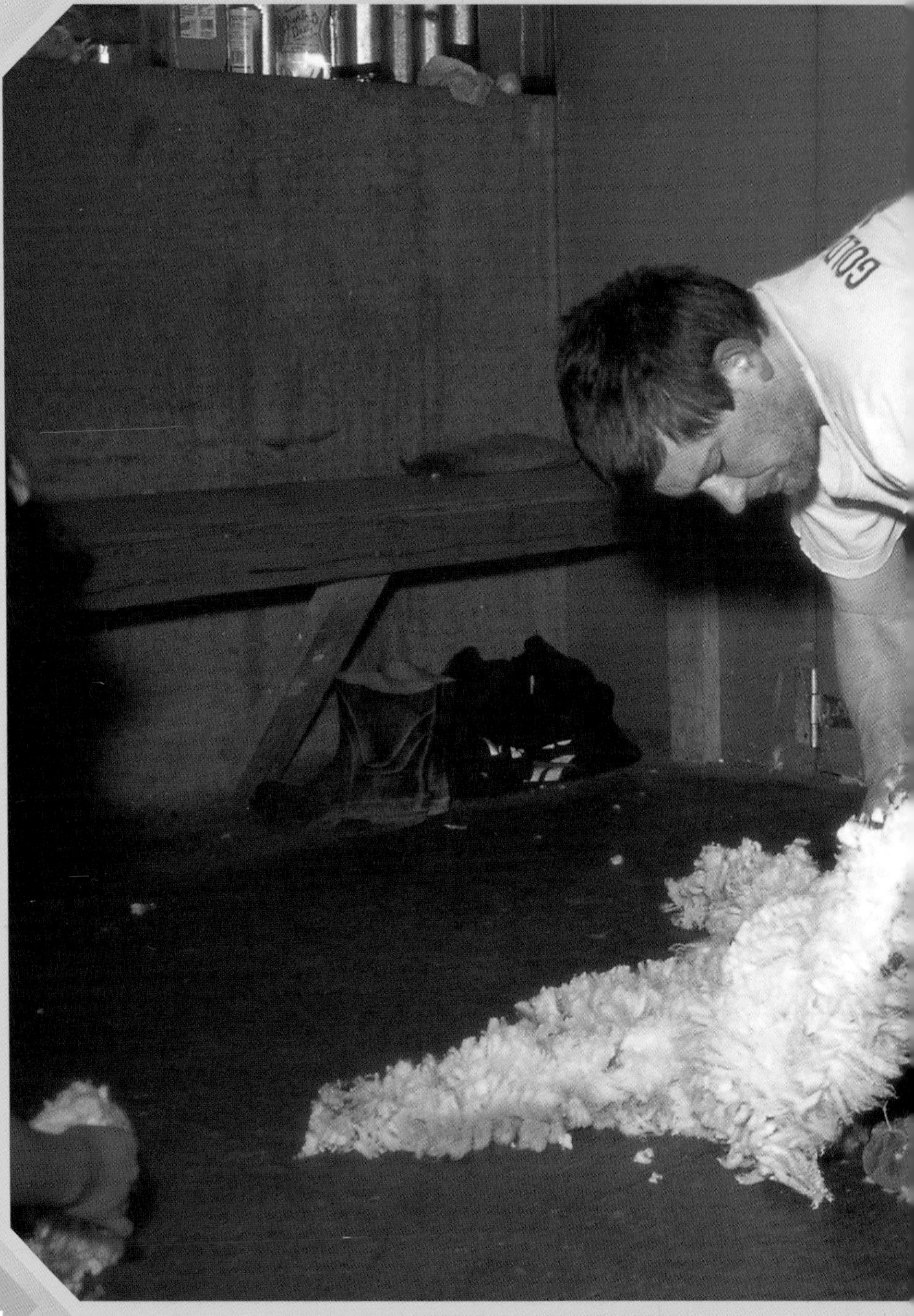

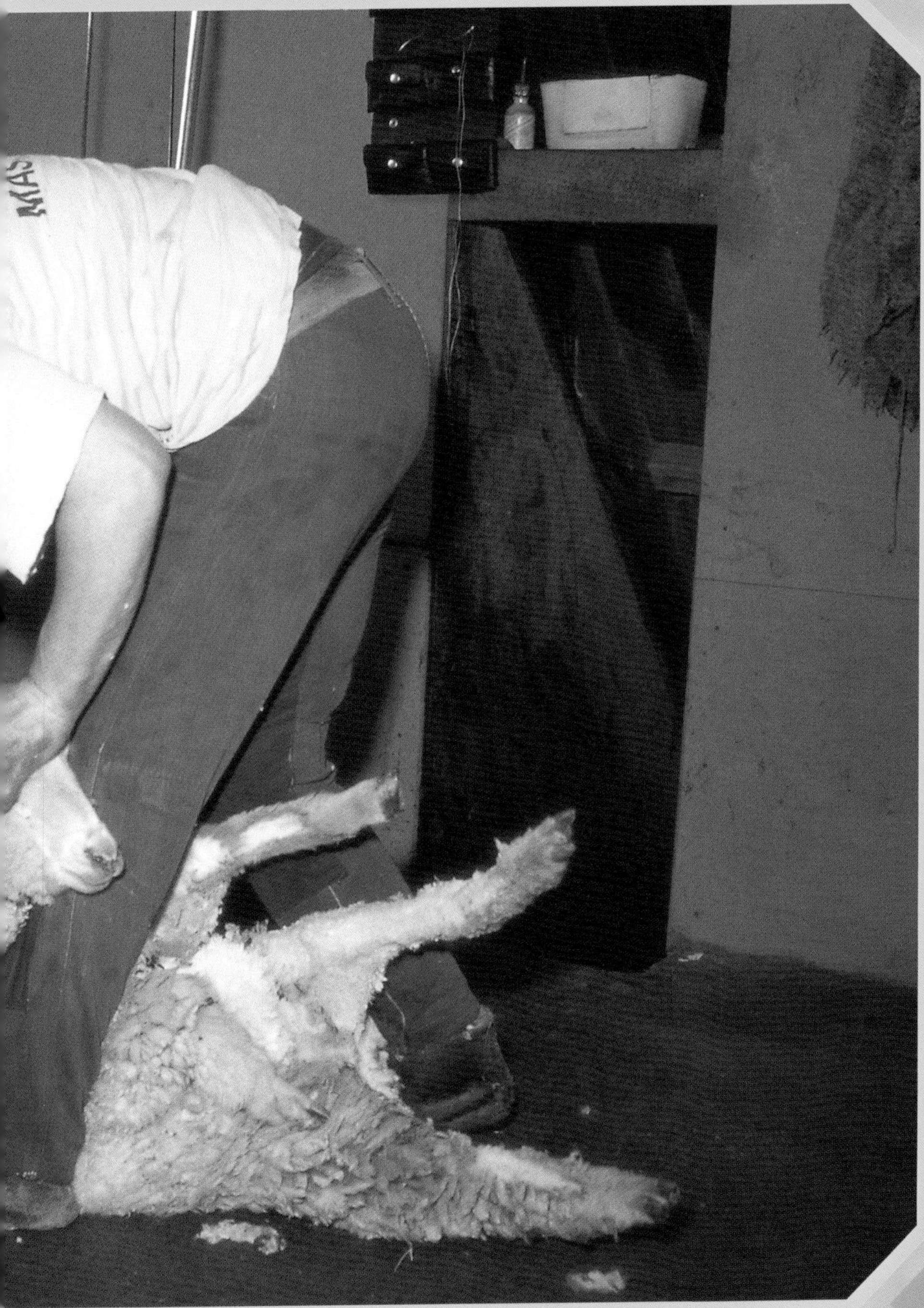

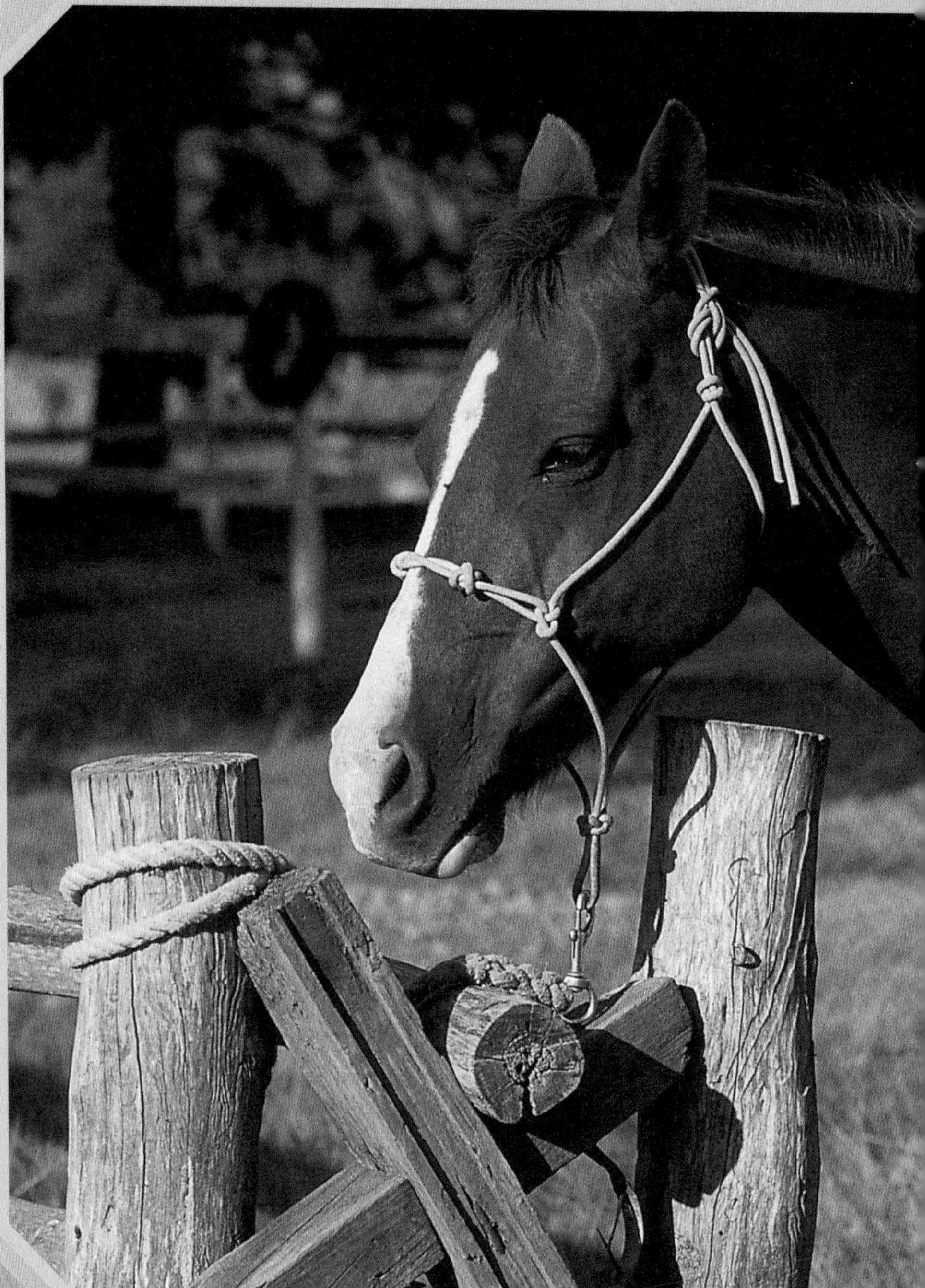

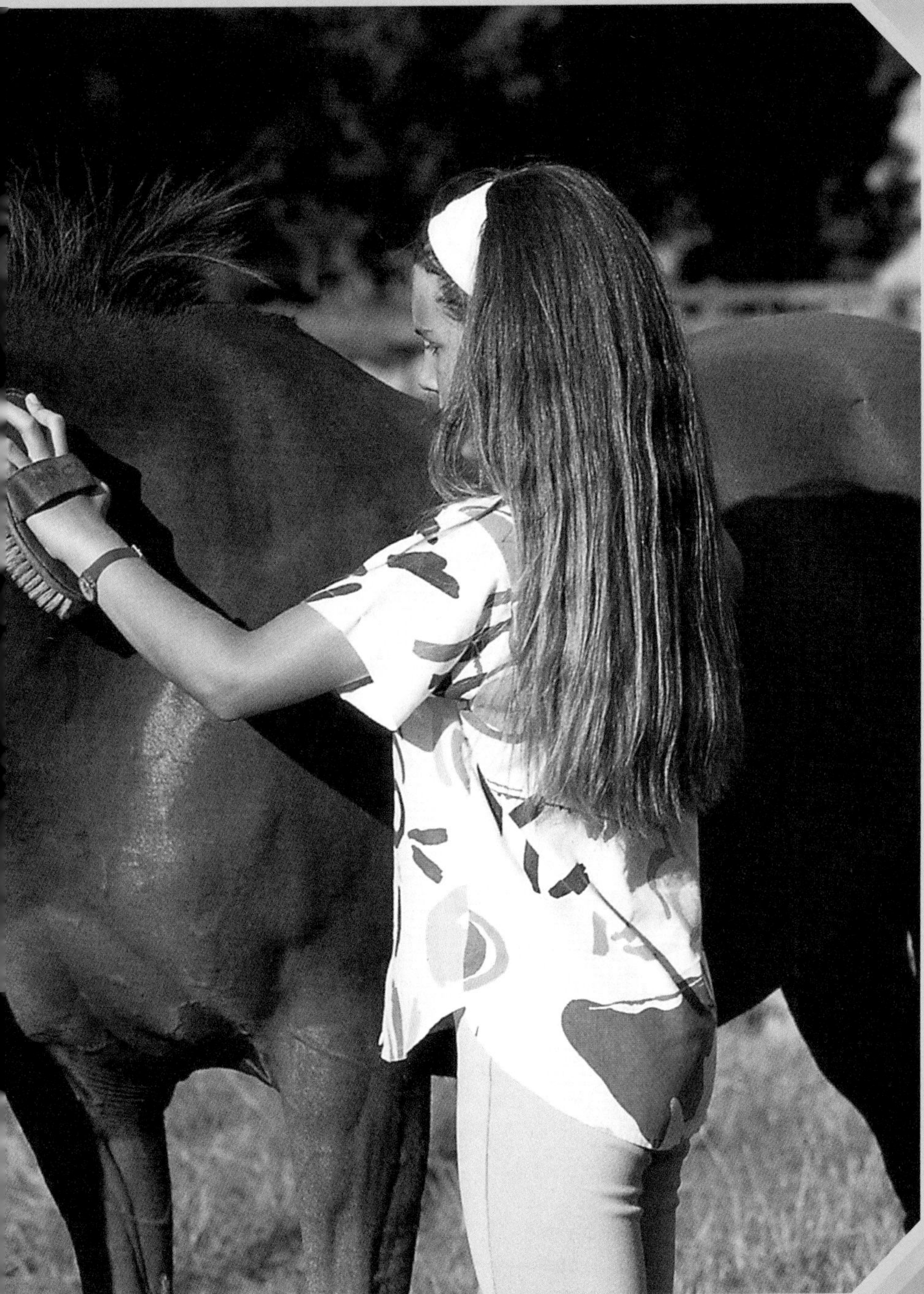

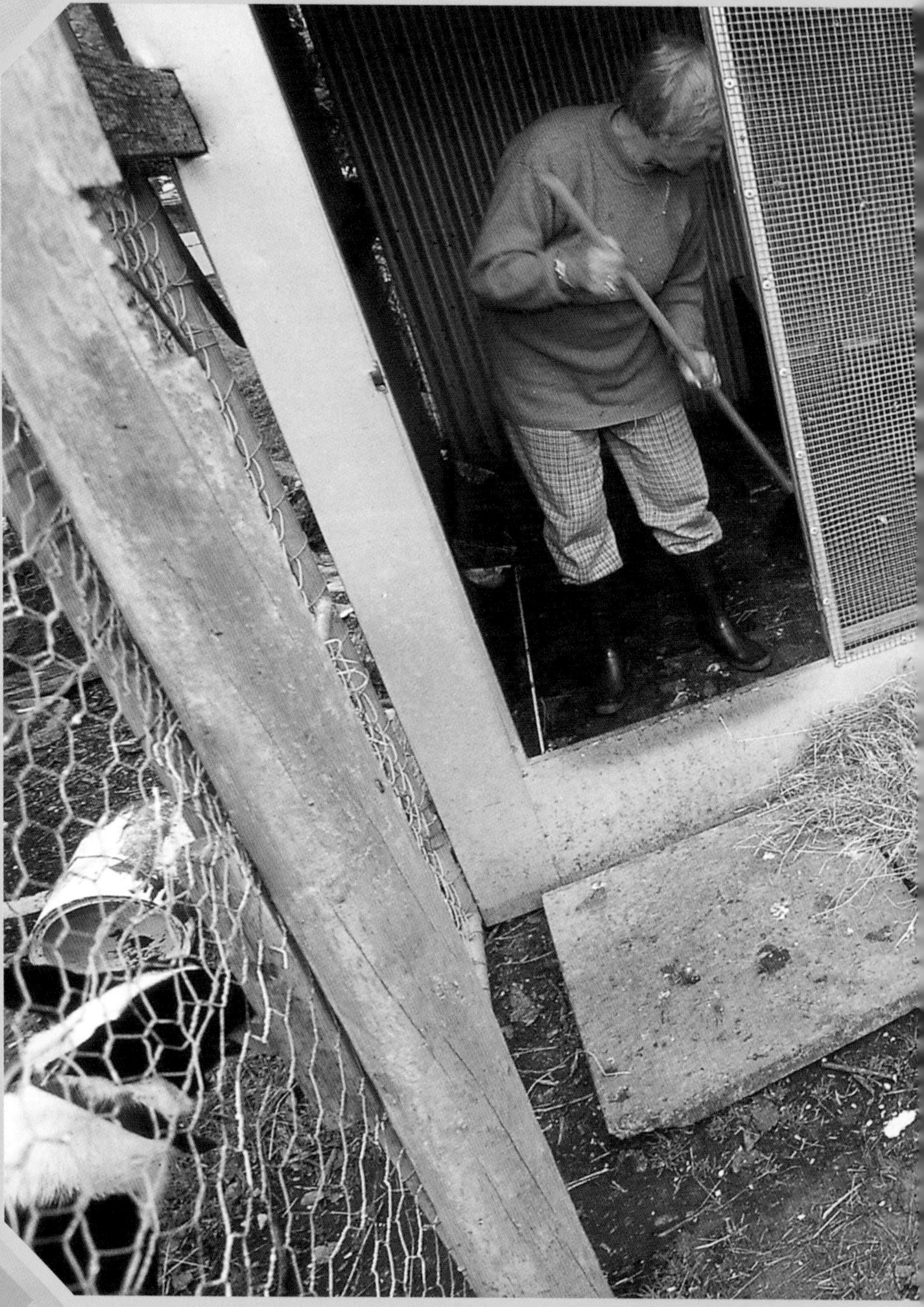

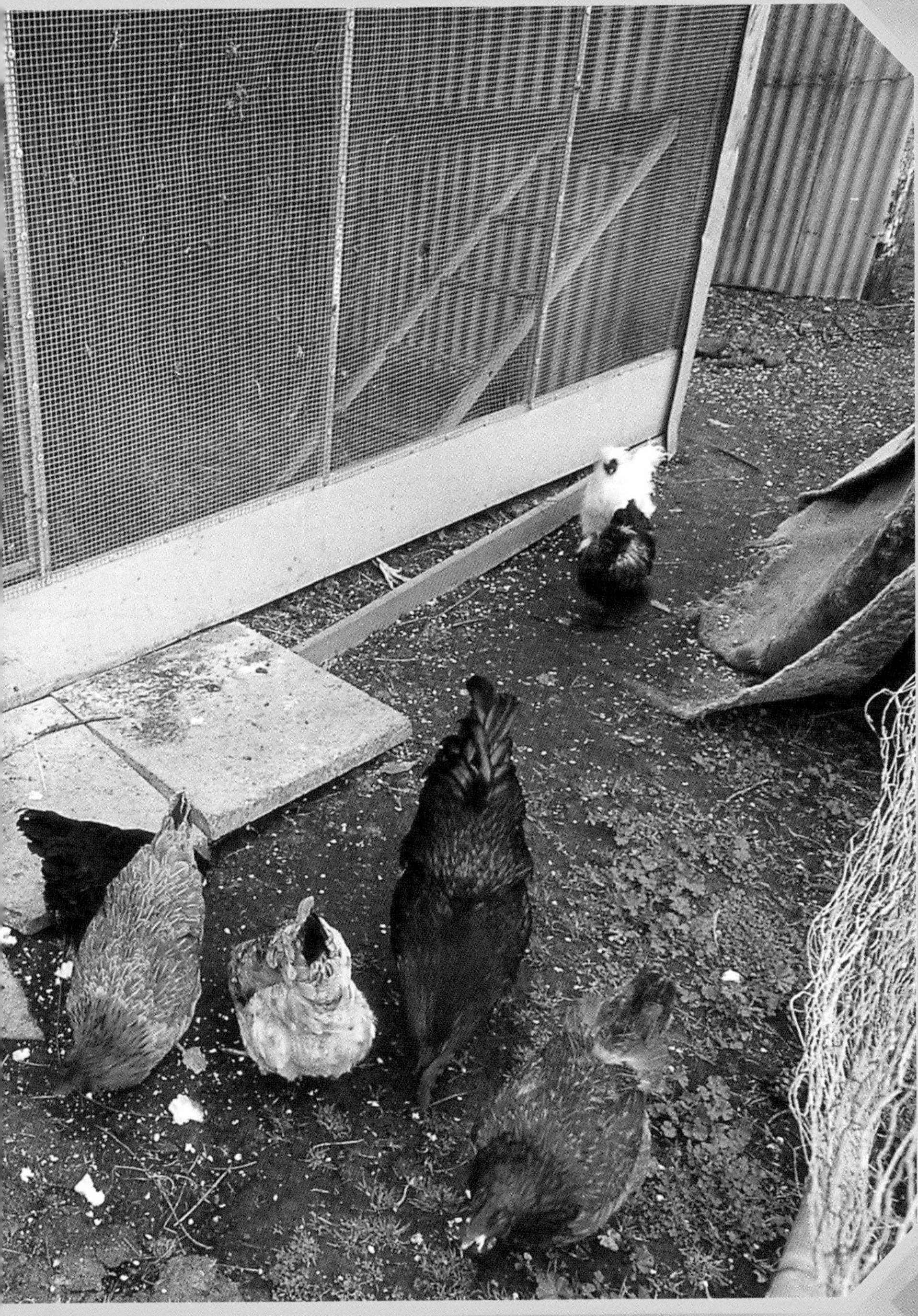

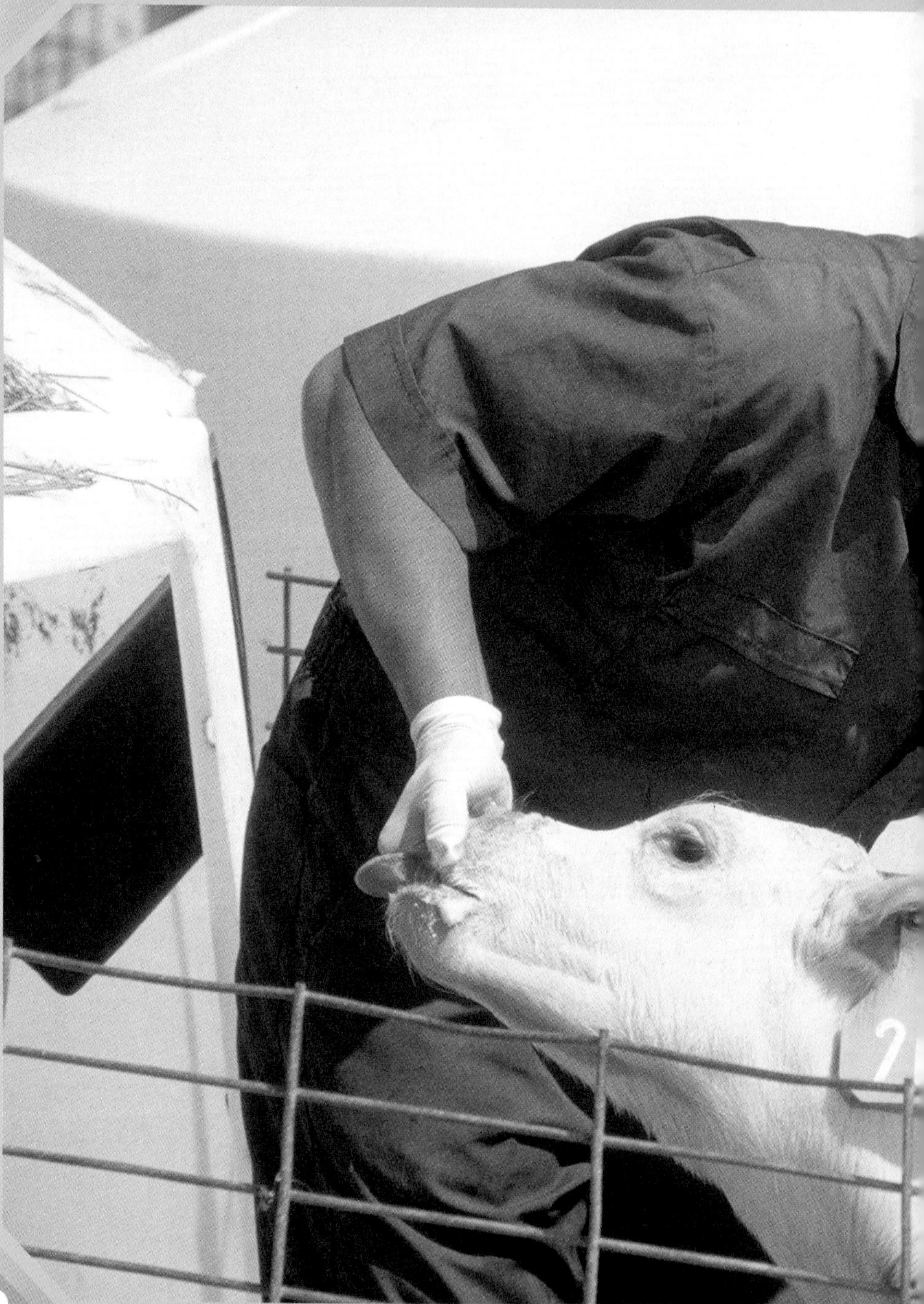

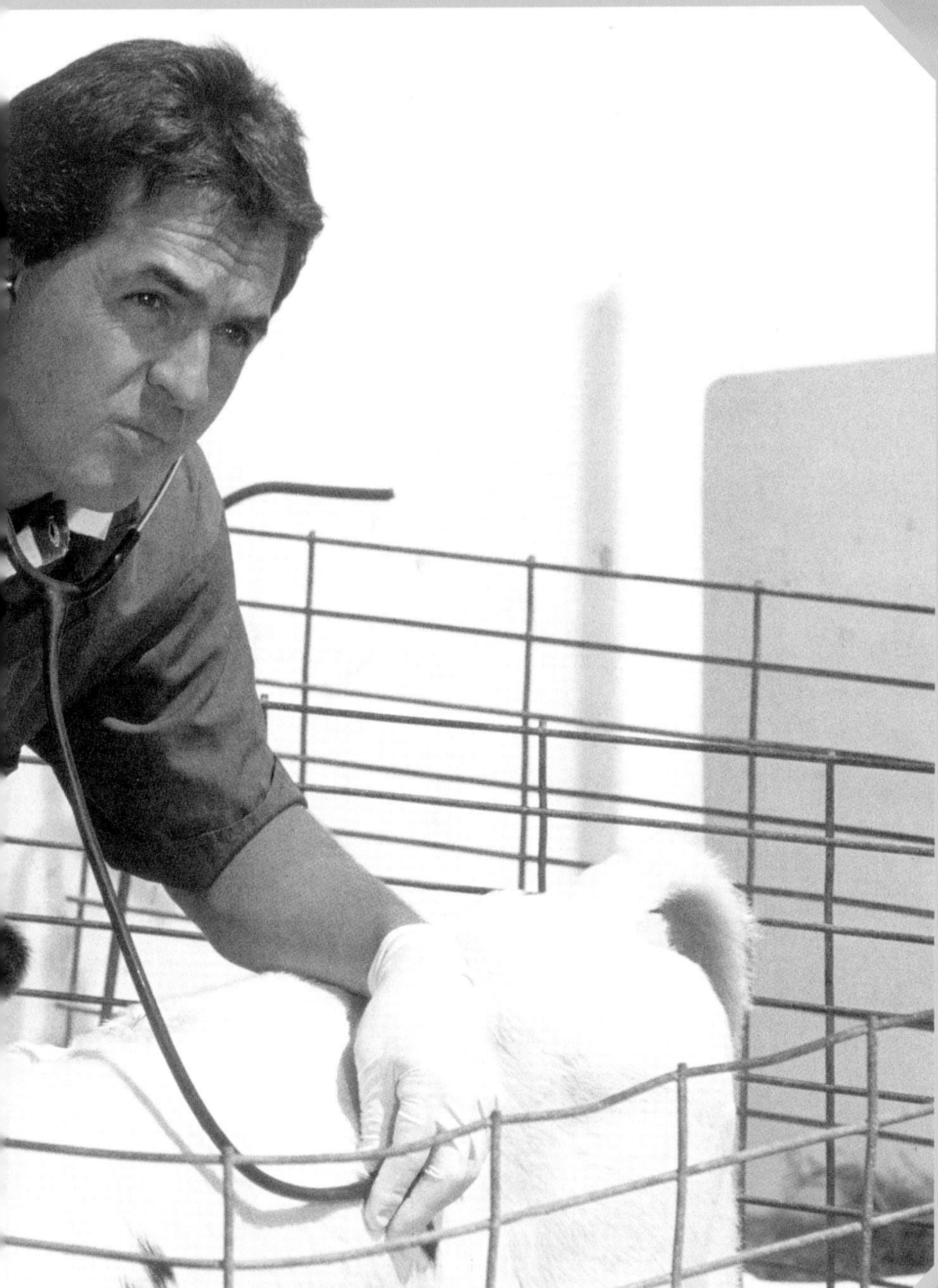

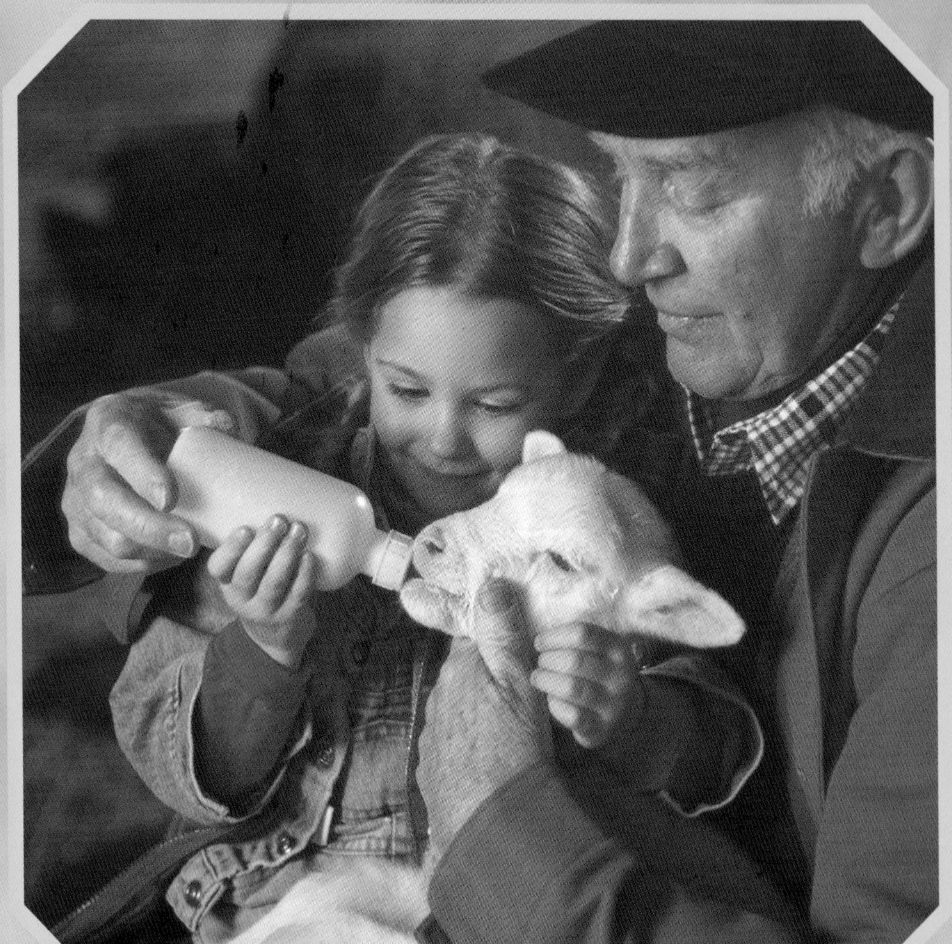